Learn To Transform
Letters Into Drawings

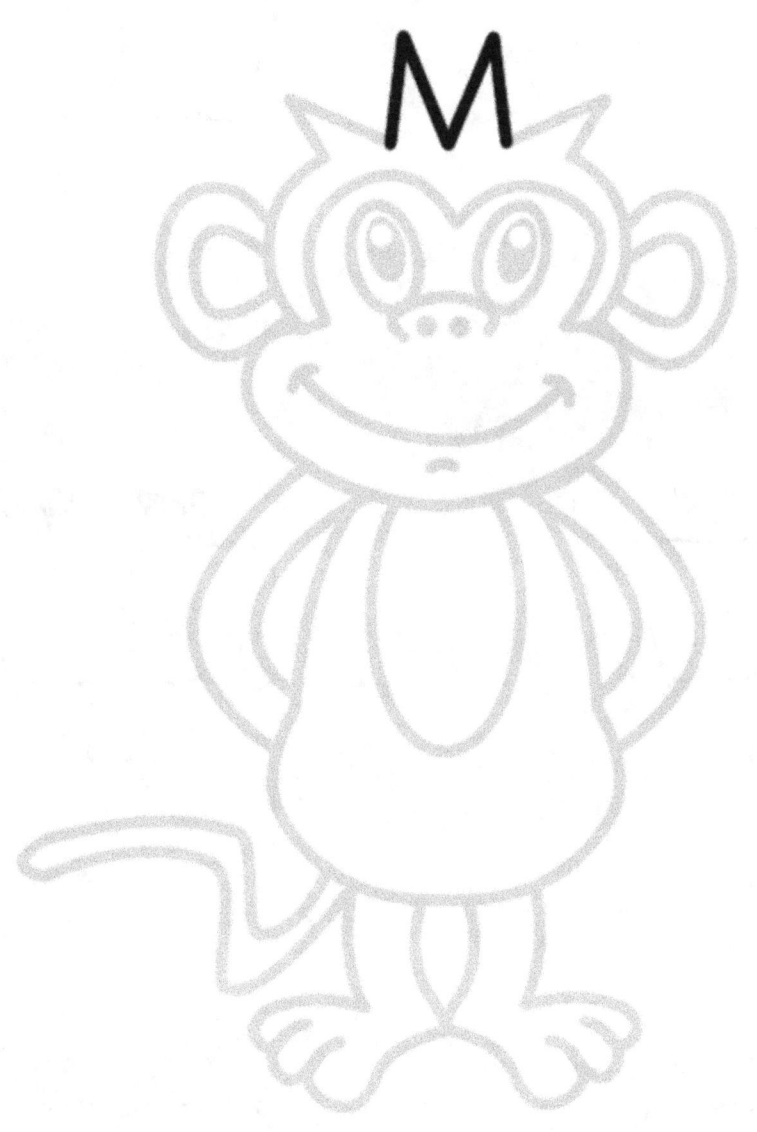

Learn the amazing transformation of all the letters of the alphabet
into creative drawings using simple and easy step-by-step guide.

Illustrated by Dexter Teope

Step by step guide to transform the letter **A** into an **Apple**.

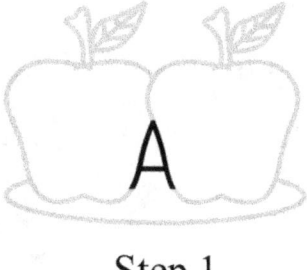

Step 1

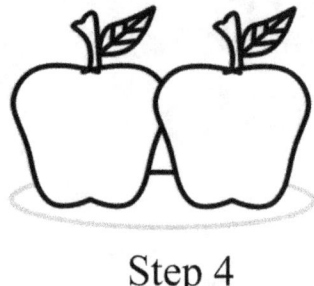

Step 4

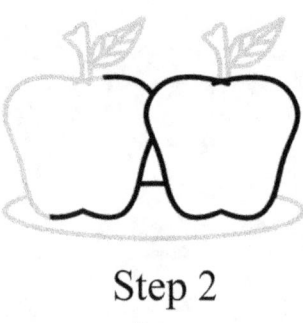

Step 2

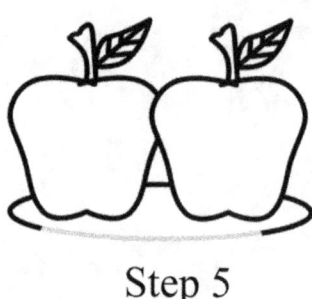

Step 5

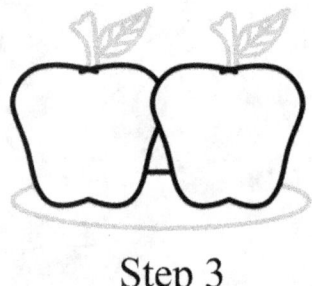

Step 3

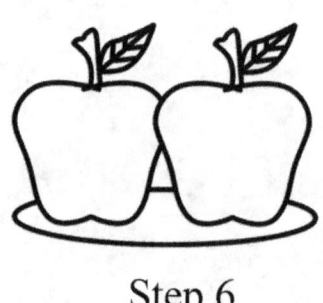

Step 6

Step by step guide to transform the letter **B** into a **Butterfly**.

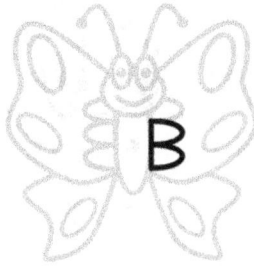

Step 1

Step 4

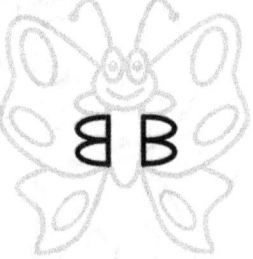

Step 2

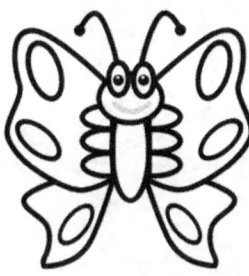

Step 5

Step 3

Step 6

Step by step guide to transform the letter **C** into a **Cat**.

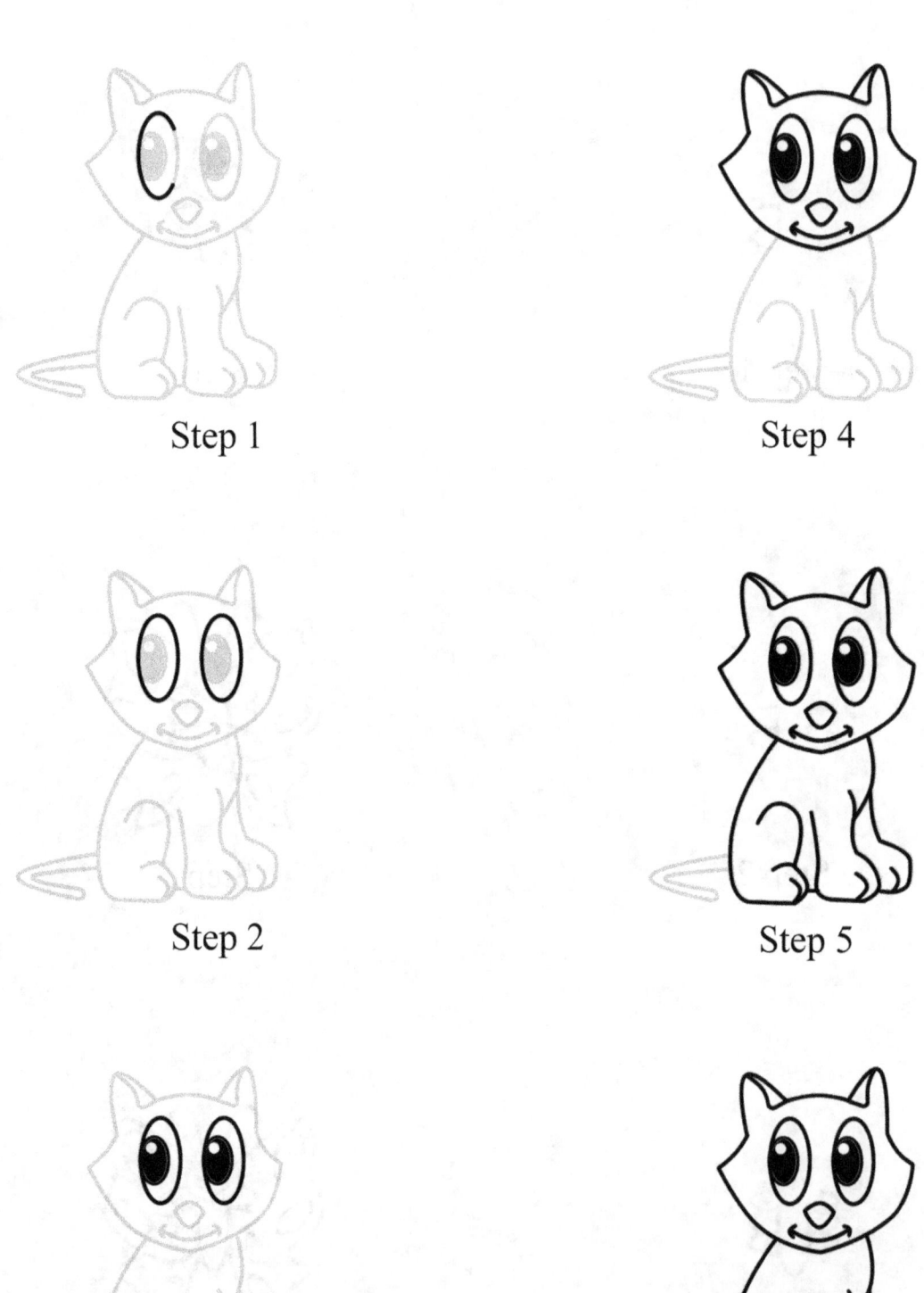

Step 1

Step 4

Step 2

Step 5

Step 3

Step 6

Step by step guide to transform the letter **D** into a **Donkey**.

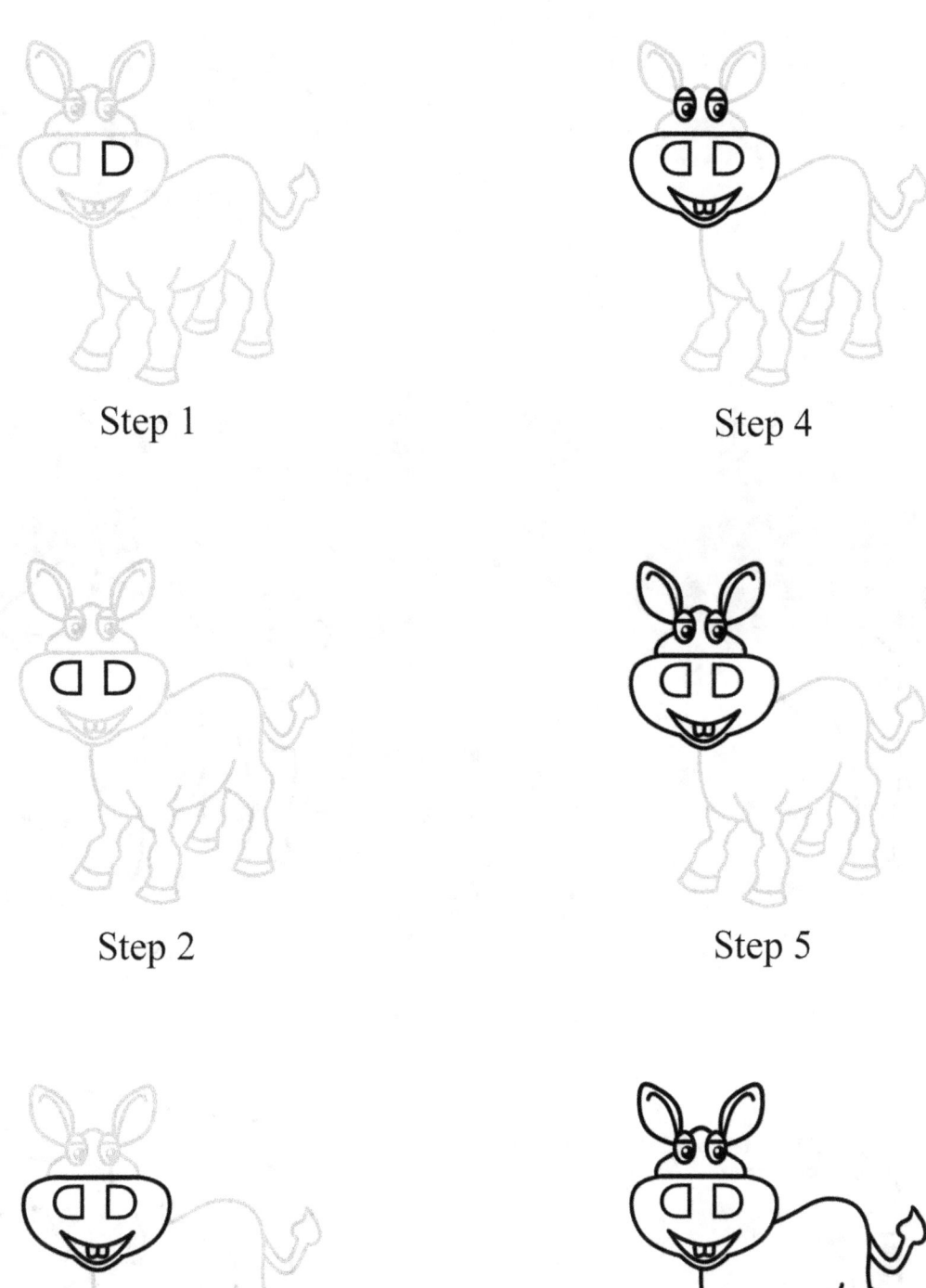

Step 1

Step 2

Step 3

Step 4

Step 5

Step 6

Step by step guide to transform the letter **E** into an **Elephant**.

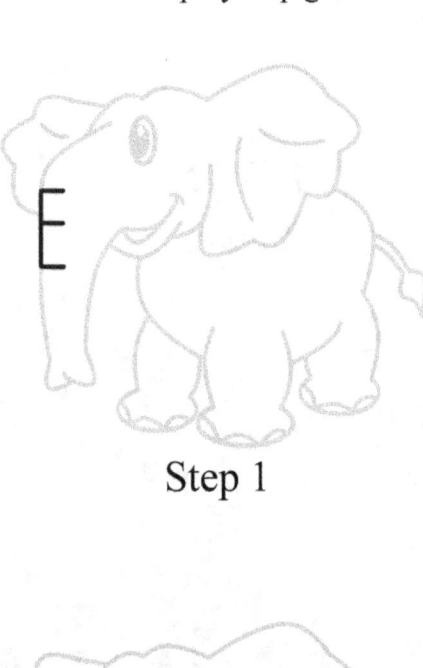

Step 1

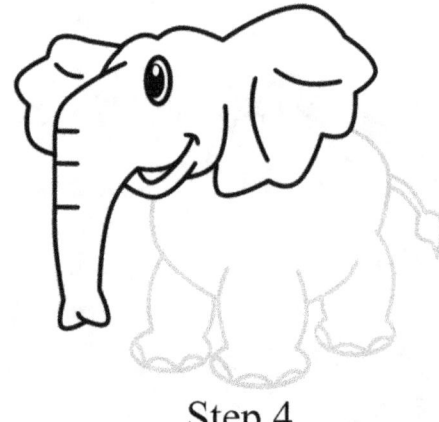

Step 4

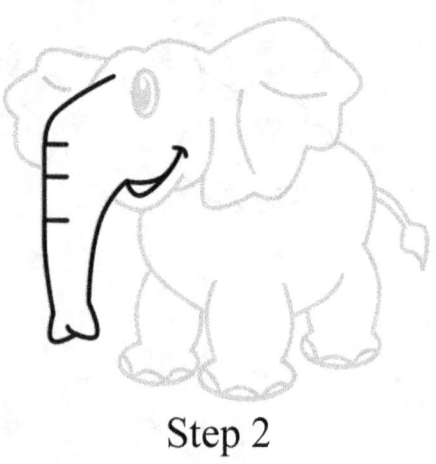

Step 2

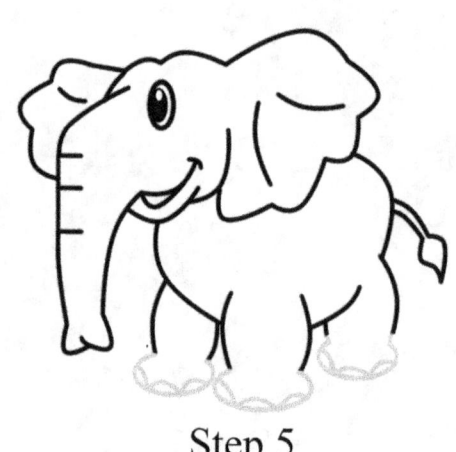

Step 5

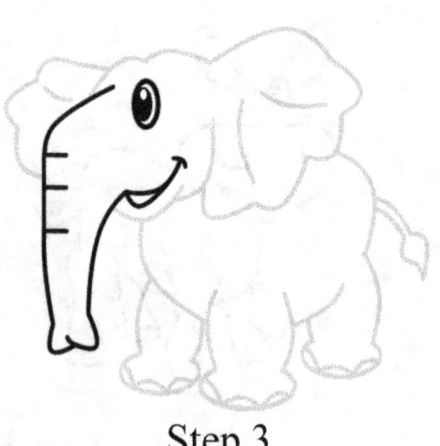

Step 3

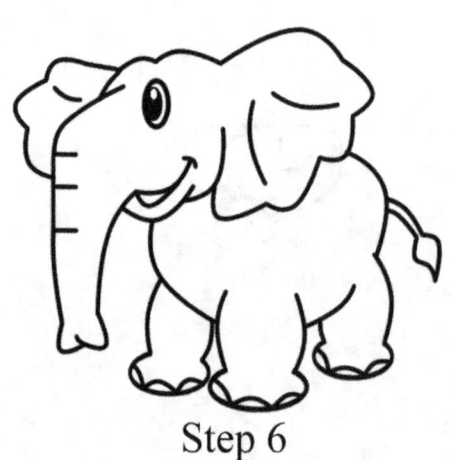

Step 6

Step by step guide to transform the letter **F** into a **Fish**.

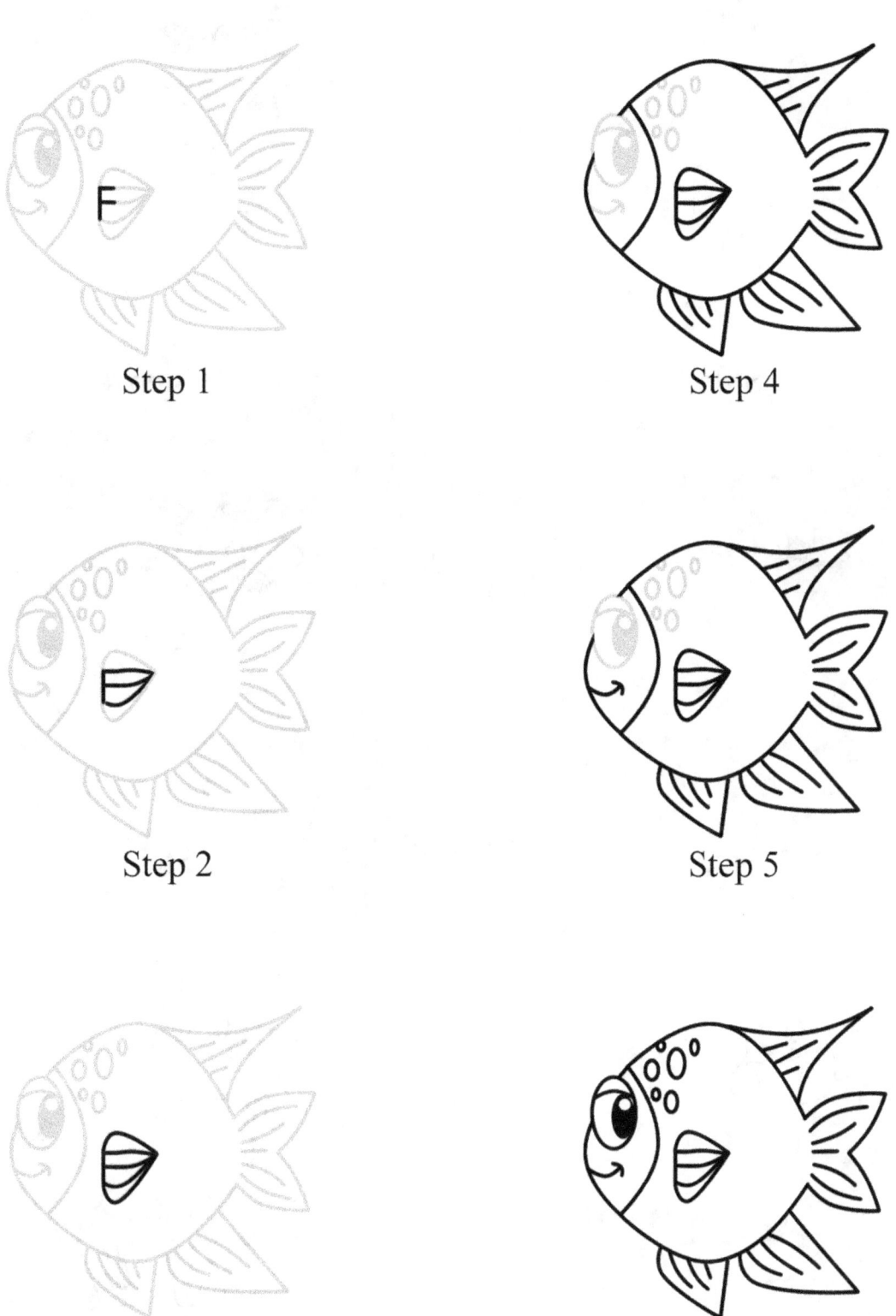

Step 1

Step 2

Step 3

Step 4

Step 5

Step 6

Step by step guide to transform the letter **G** into a **Goat**.

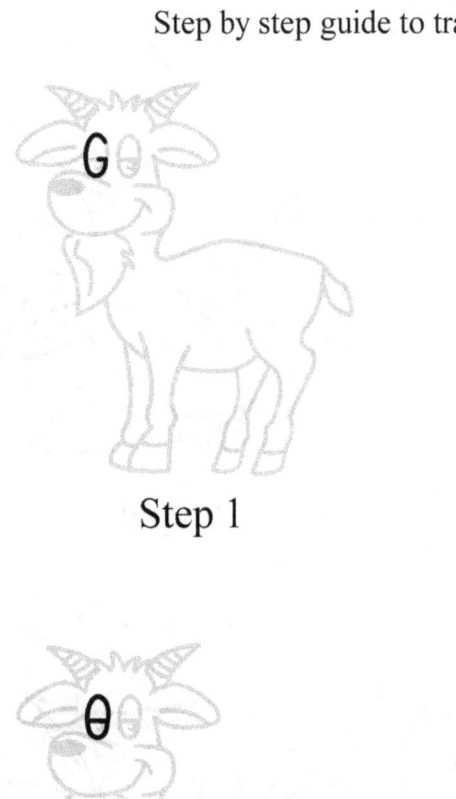

Step 1

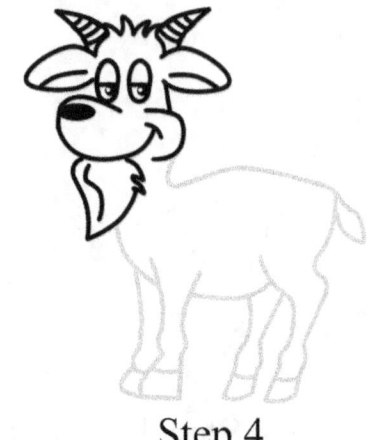
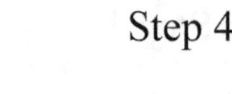

Step 4

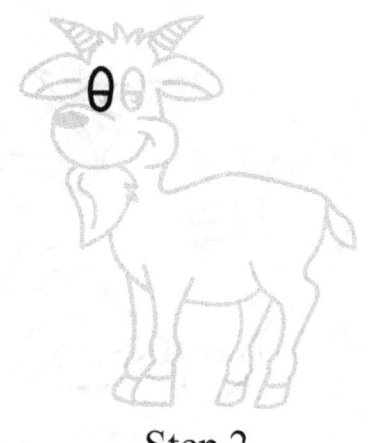

Step 2

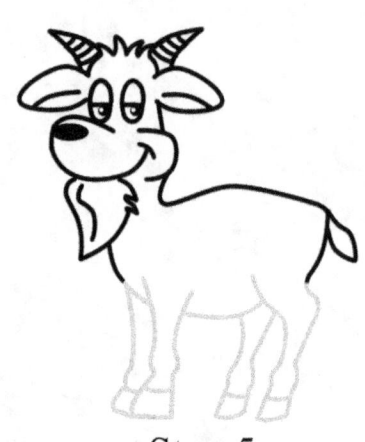

Step 5

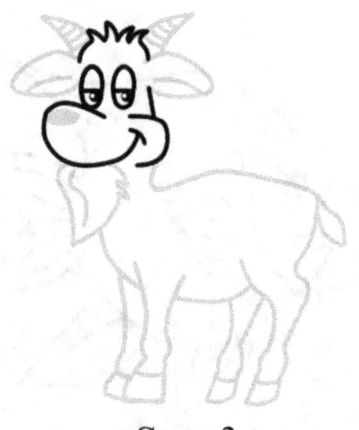

Step 3

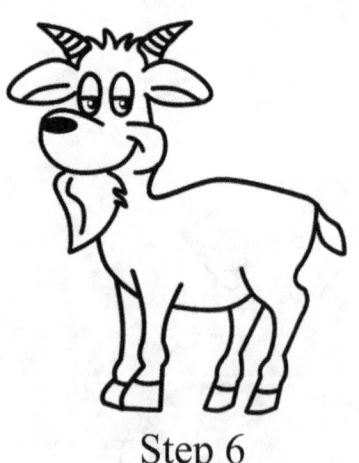

Step 6

Step by step guide to transform the letter **H** into a **Hipopotamus**.

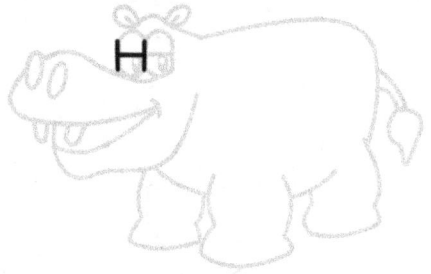

Step 1

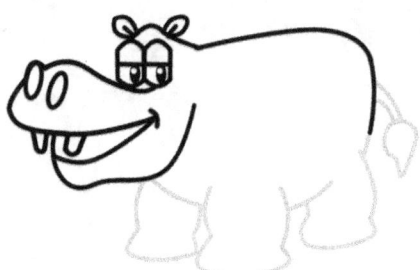

Step 4

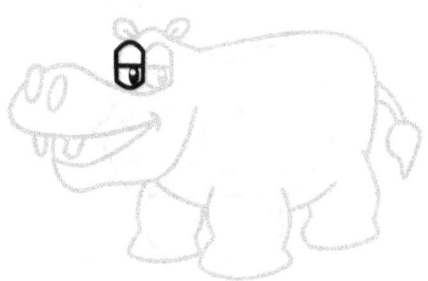

Step 2

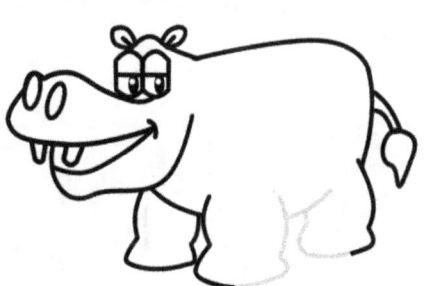

Step 5

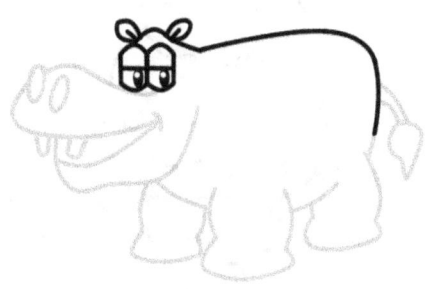

Step 3

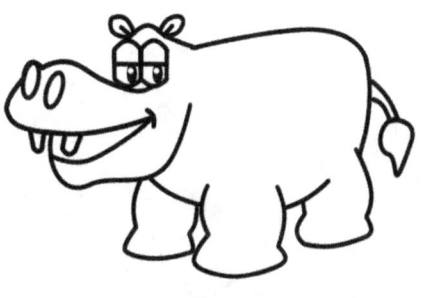

Step 6

Step by step guide to transform the letter **I** into an **Ice Cream**.

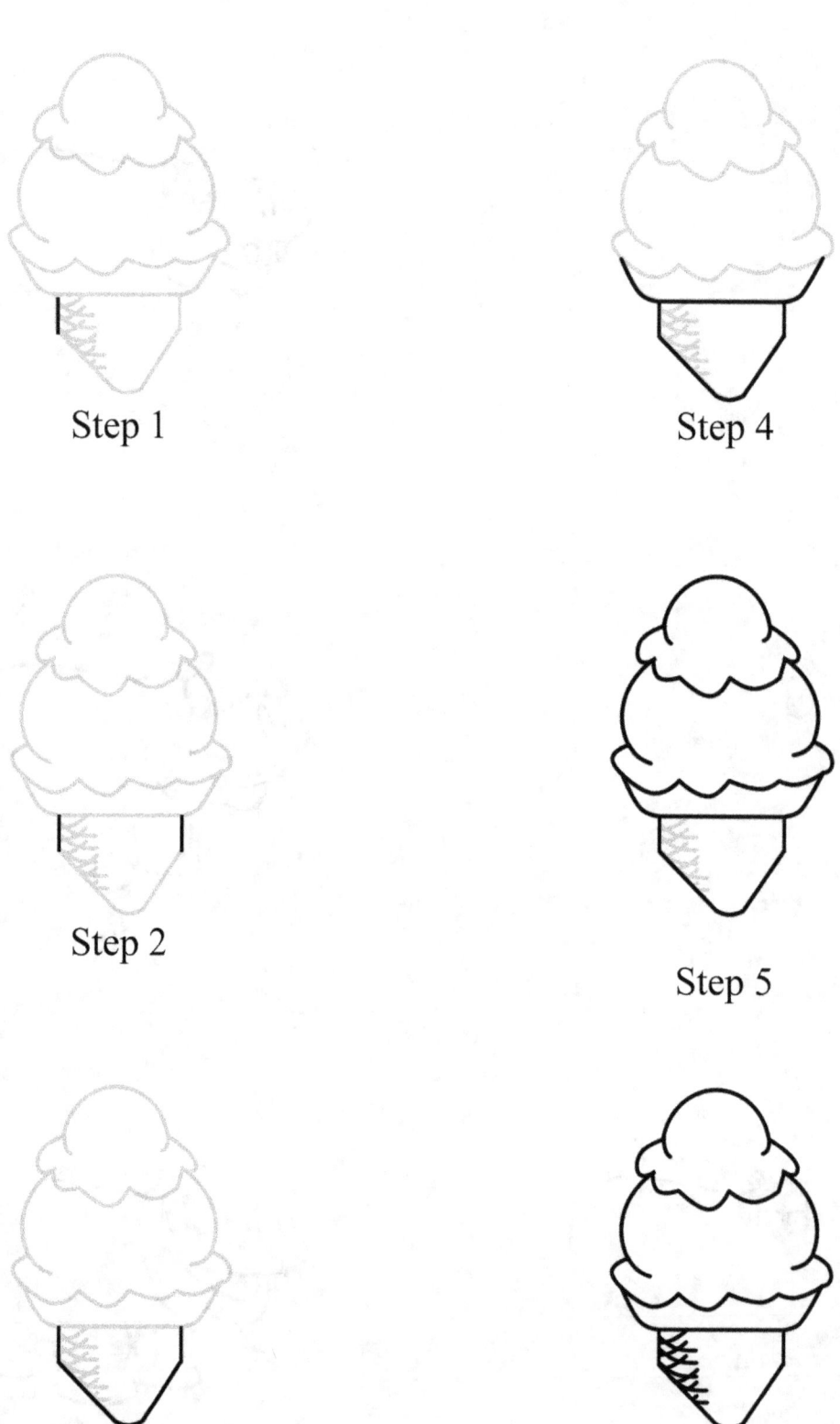

Step 1

Step 2

Step 3

Step 4

Step 5

Step 6

Step by step guide to transform the letter **J** into a **Jellyfish**.

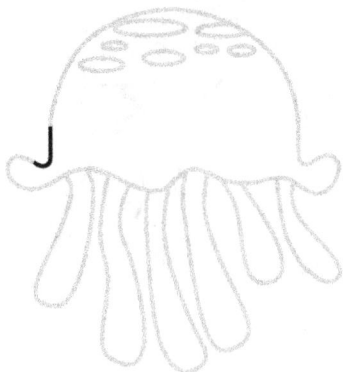

Step 1

Step 4

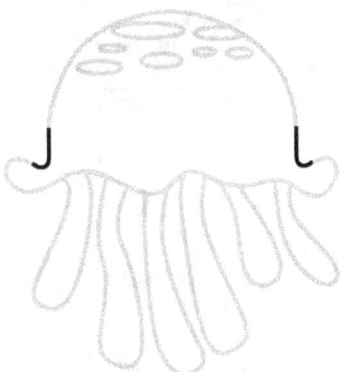

Step 2

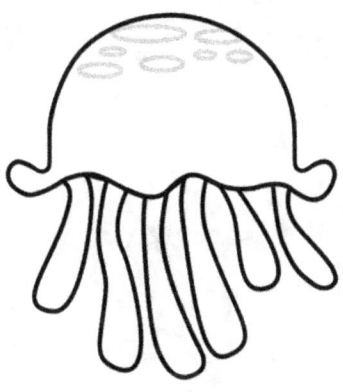

Step 5

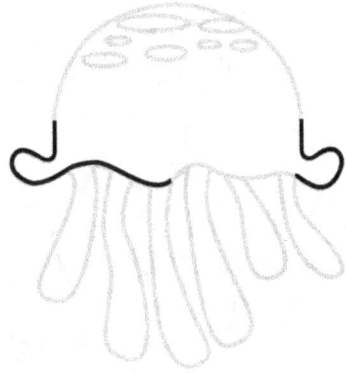

Step 3

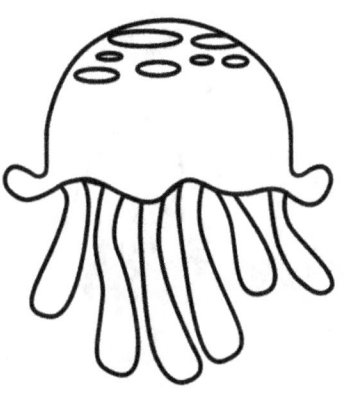

Step 6

Step by step guide to transform the letter **K** into a **Kangaroo**.

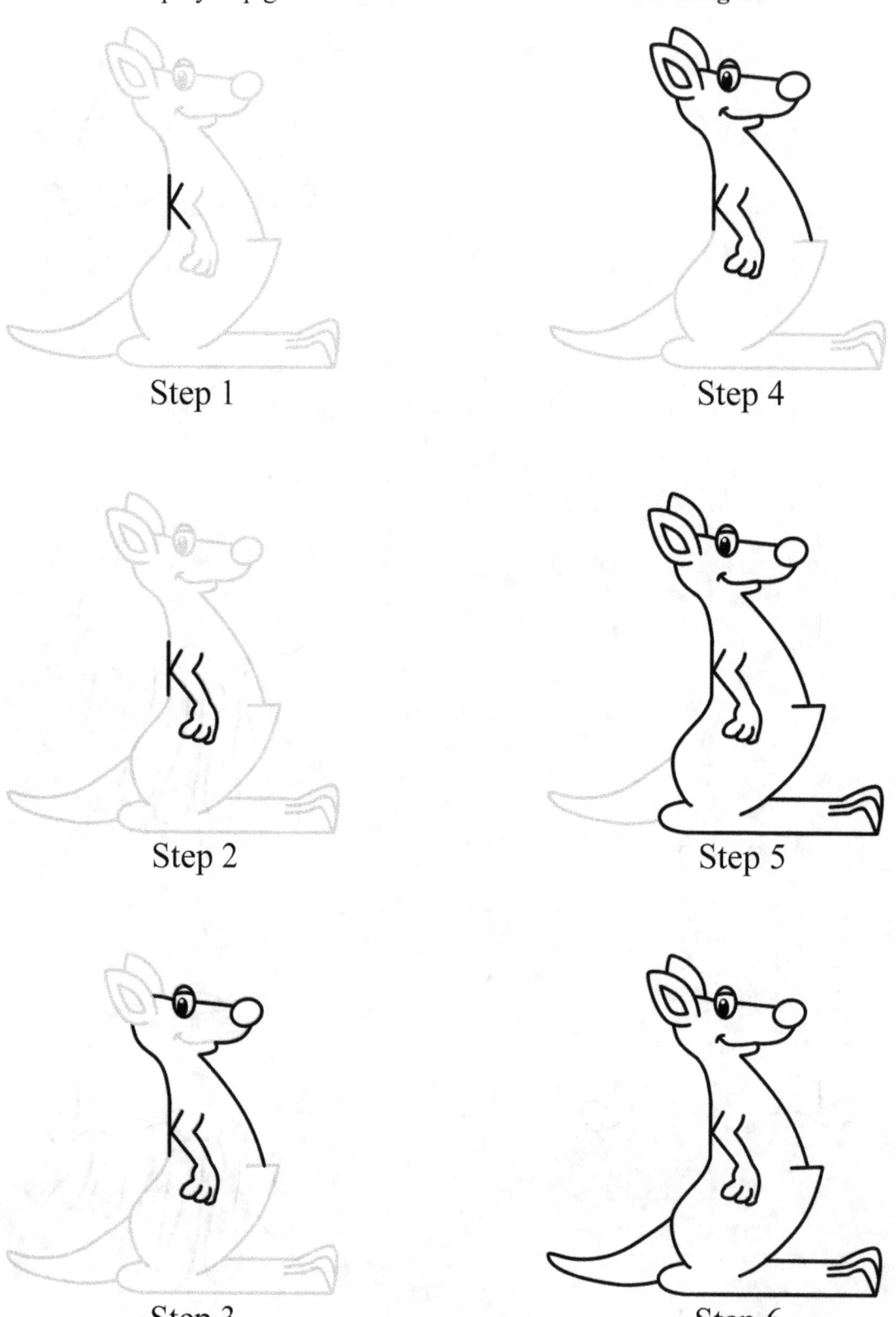

Step 1

Step 2

Step 3

Step 4

Step 5

Step 6

Step by step guide to transform the letter **L** into a **Lion**.

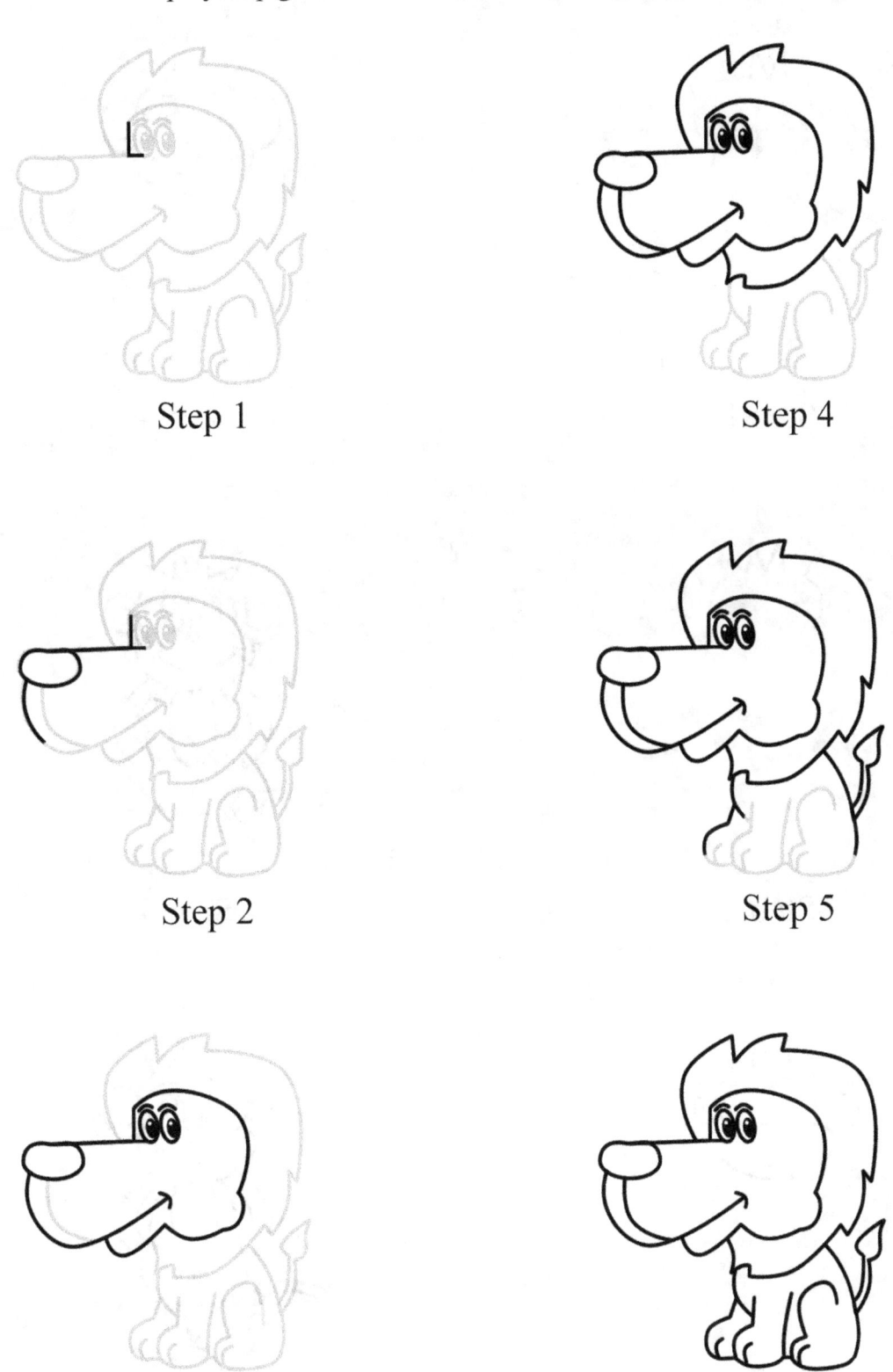

Step 1

Step 2

Step 3

Step 4

Step 5

Step 6

Step by step guide to transform the letter **M** into a **Monkey**.

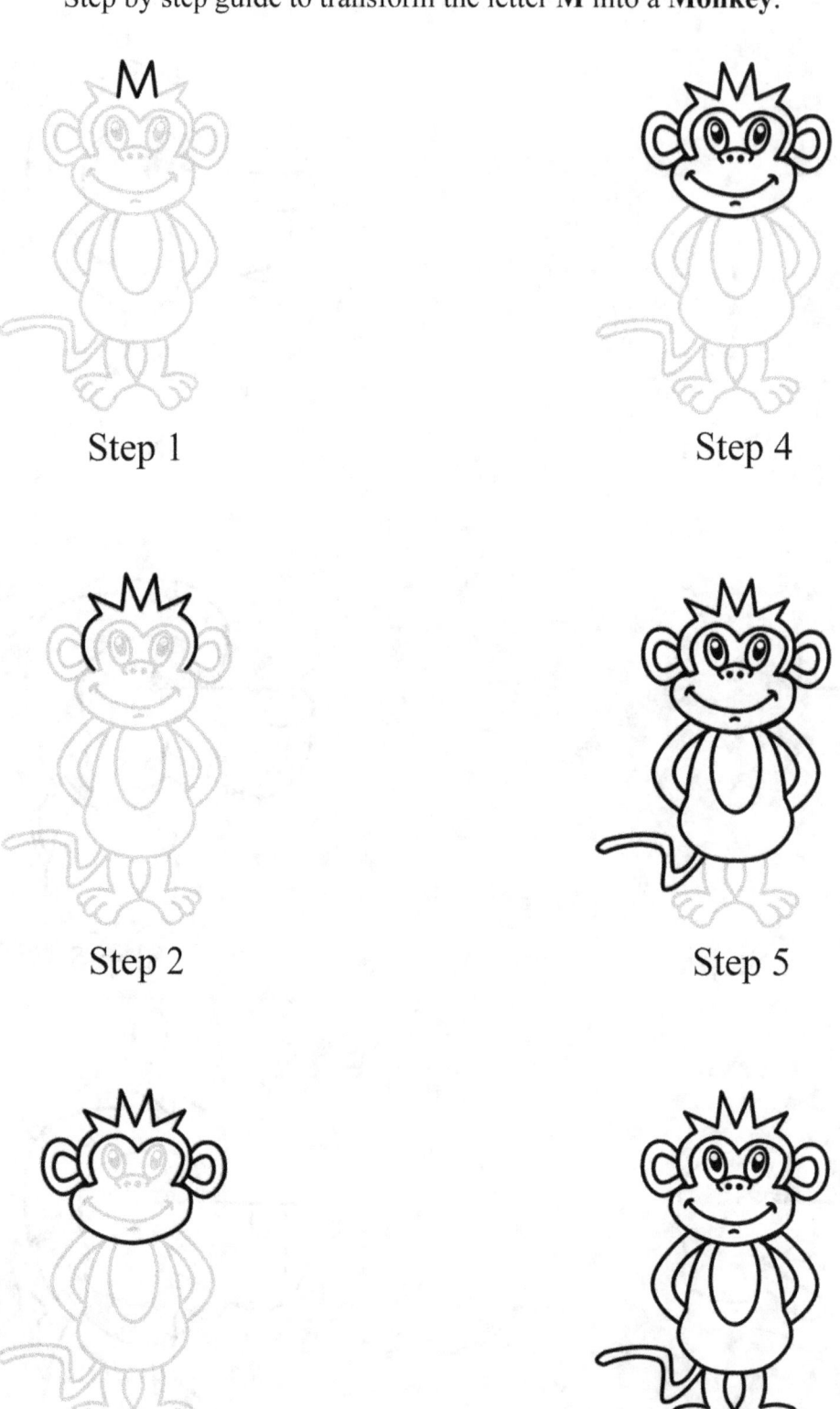

Step 1

Step 2

Step 3

Step 4

Step 5

Step 6

Step by step guide to transform the letter **N** into a **Nose**.

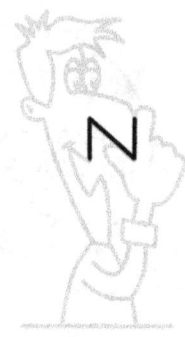

Step 1

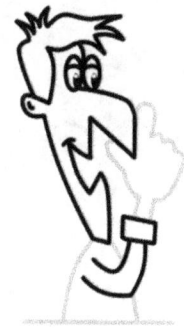

Step 4

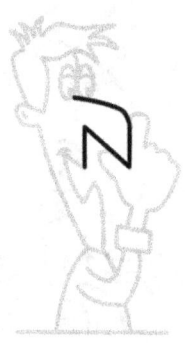

Step 2

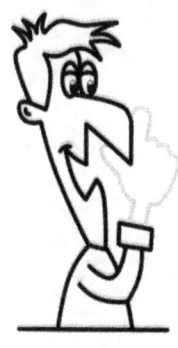

Step 5

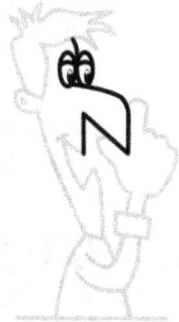

Step 3

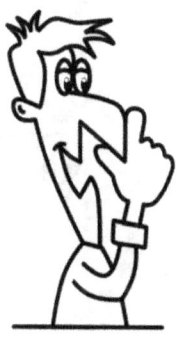

Step 6

Step by step guide to transform the letter **O** into an **Octupus**.

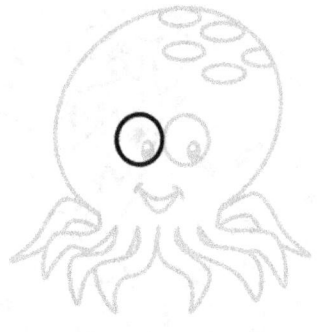

Step 1

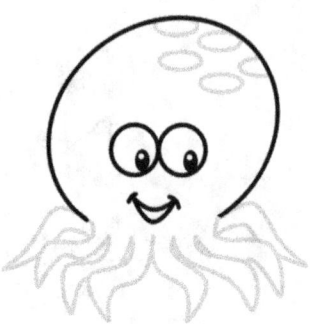

Step 4

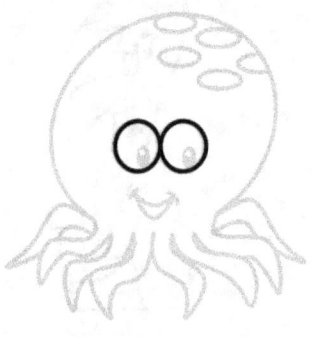

Step 2

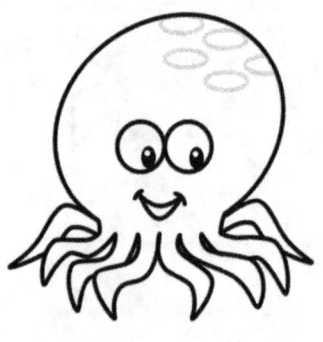

Step 5

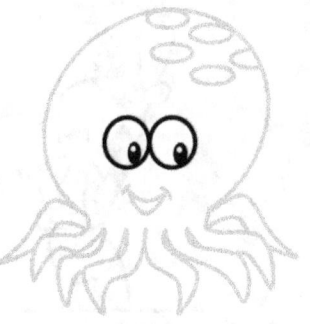

Step 3

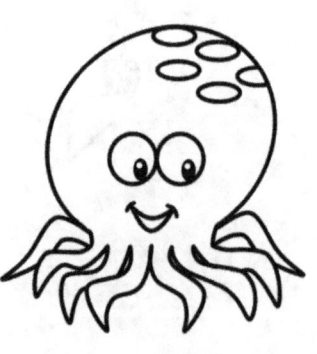

Step 6

Step by step guide to transform the letter **P** into a **Penguin**.

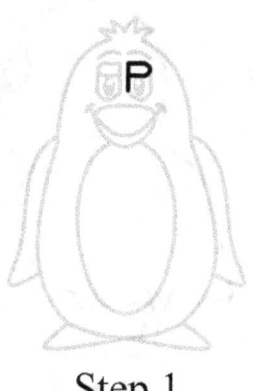

Step 1

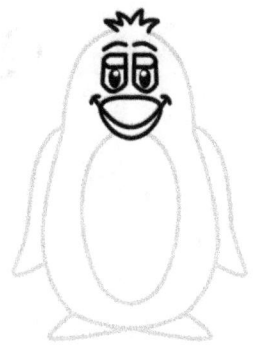

Step 4

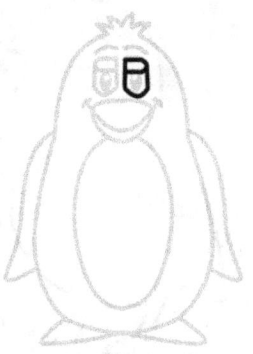

Step 2

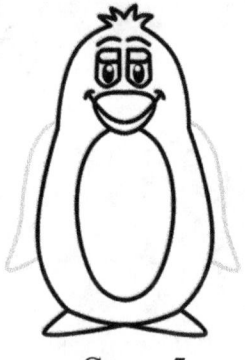

Step 5

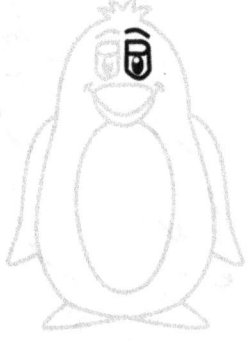

Step 3

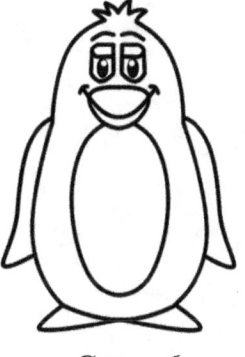

Step 6

Step by step guide to transform the letter **Q** into a **Quail**.

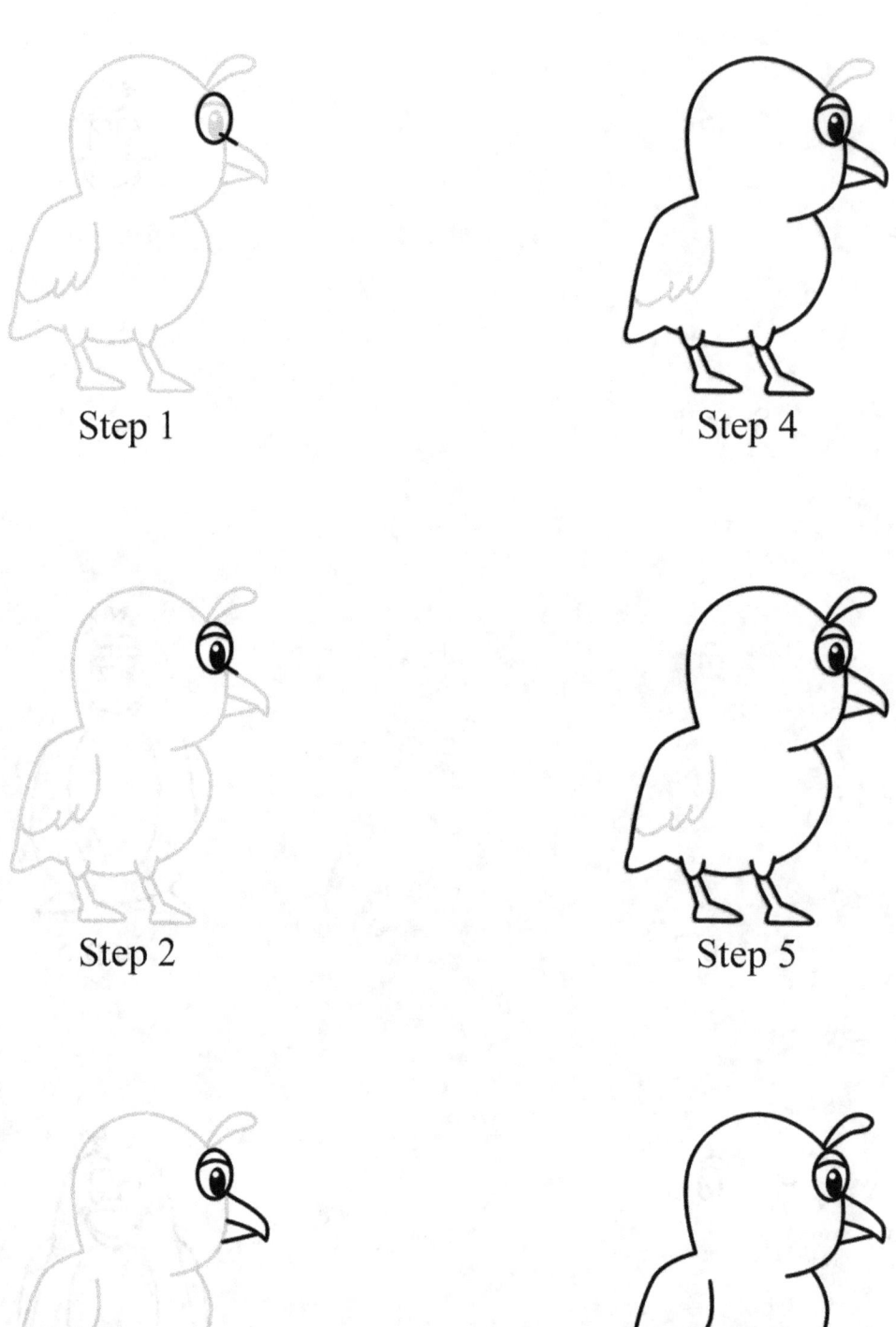

Step 1

Step 2

Step 3

Step 4

Step 5

Step 6

Step by step guide to transform the letter **R** into a **Rabbit**.

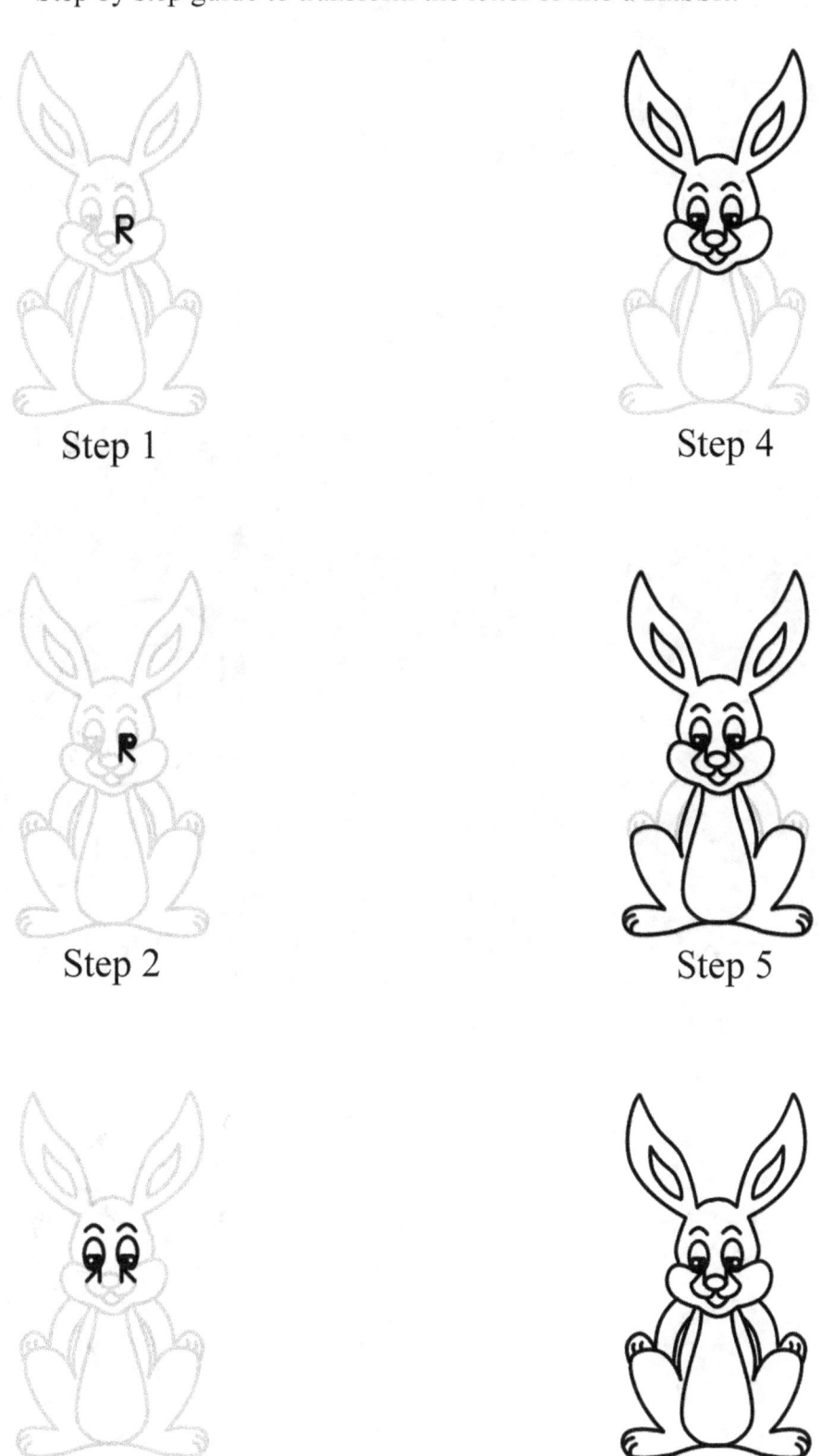

Step 1

Step 2

Step 3

Step 4

Step 5

Step 6

Step by step guide to transform the letter **S** into a **Snake**.

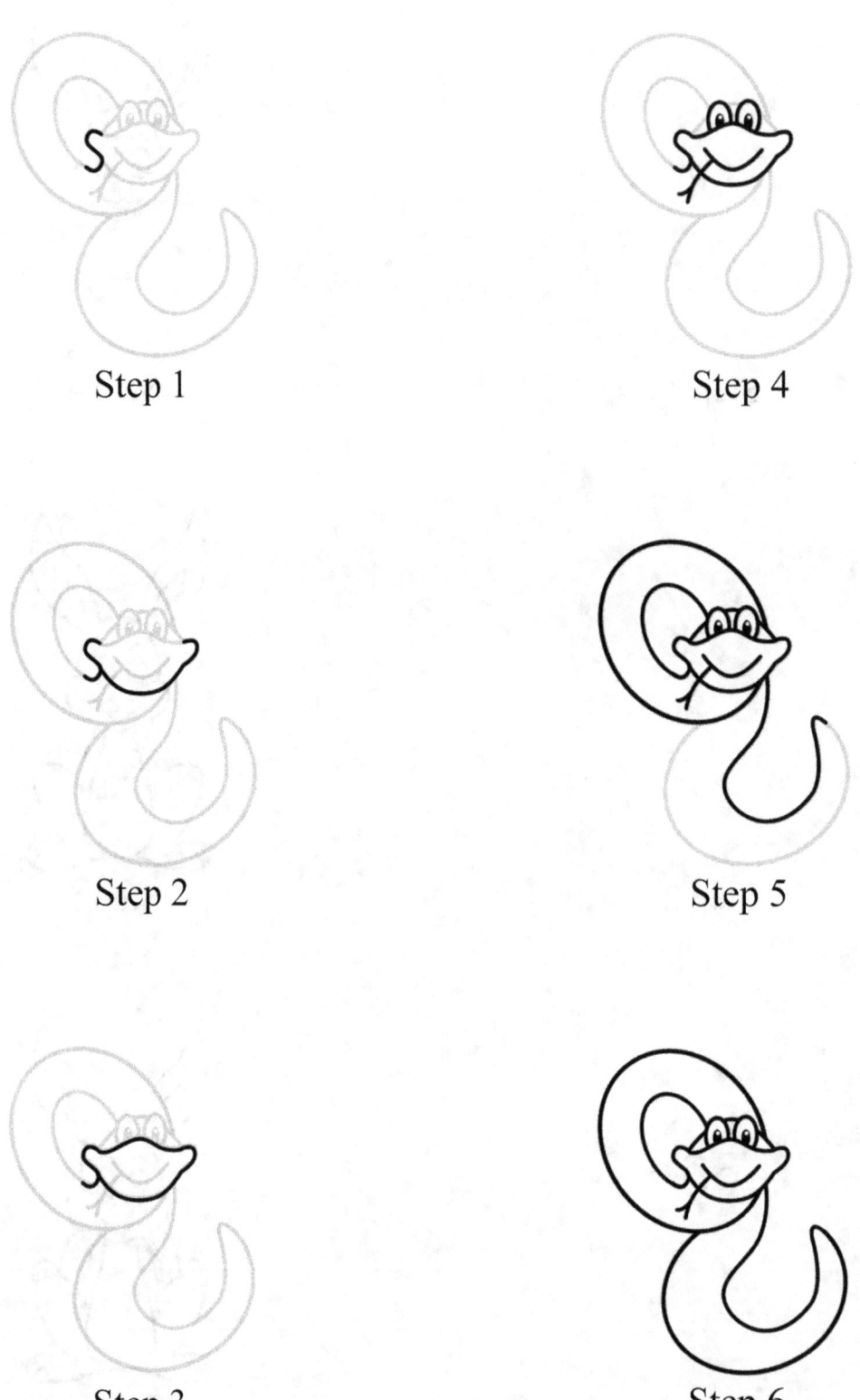

Step 1

Step 2

Step 3

Step 4

Step 5

Step 6

Step by step guide to transform the letter **T** into a **Turkey**.

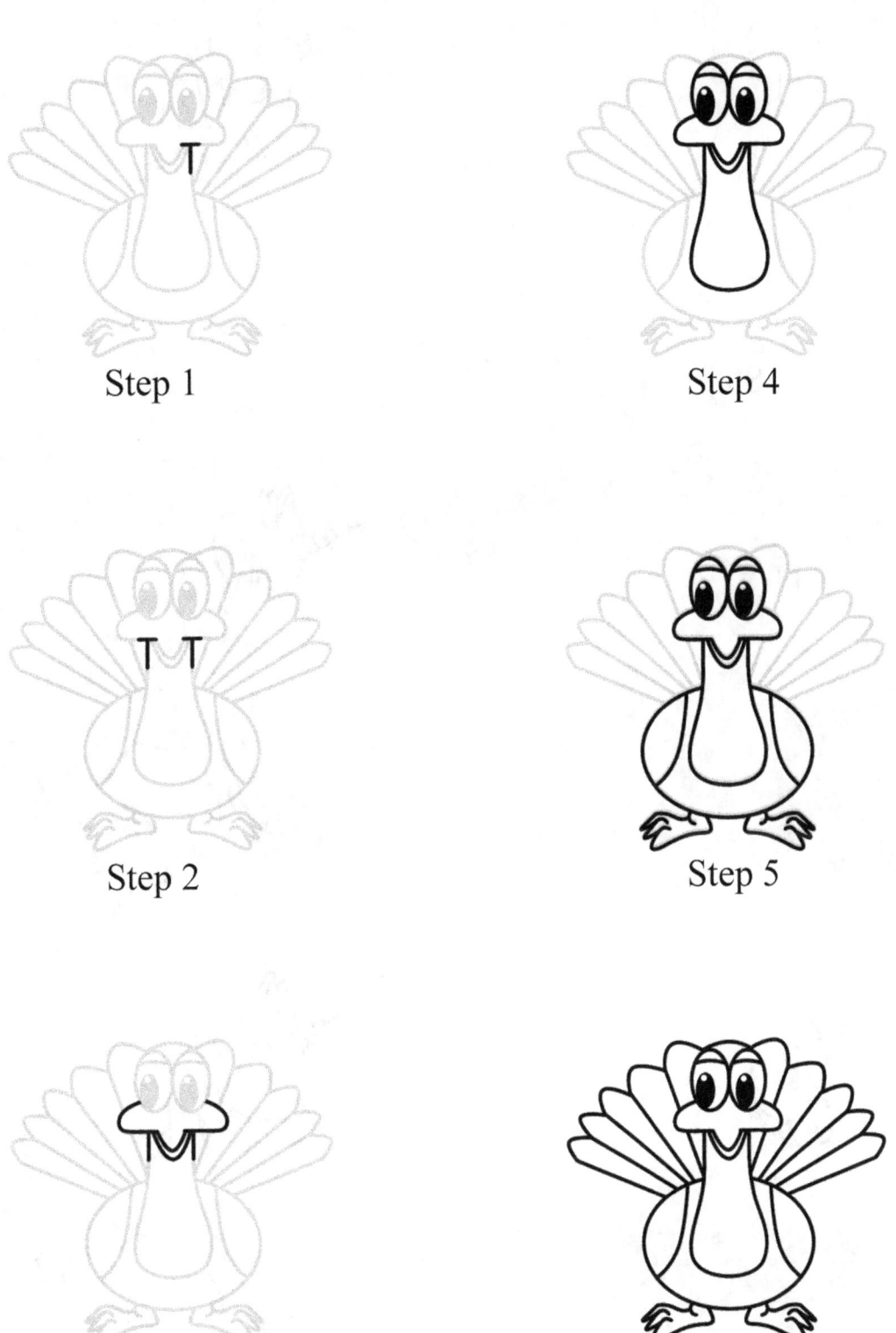

Step 1

Step 2

Step 3

Step 4

Step 5

Step 6

Step by step guide to transform the letter **U** into an **Unicorn**.

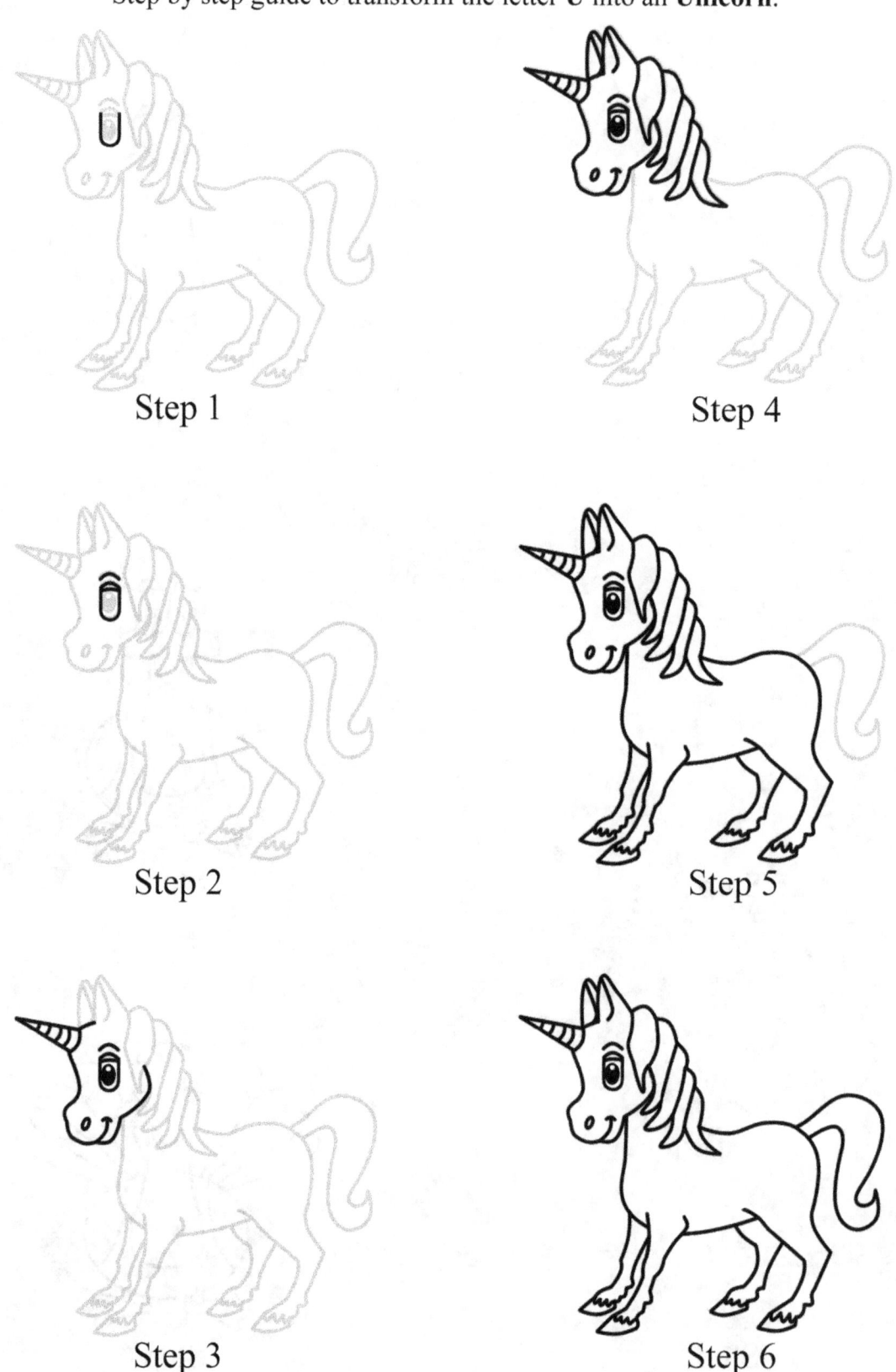

Step 1

Step 4

Step 2

Step 5

Step 3

Step 6

Step by step guide to transform the letter **V** into a **Vulture**.

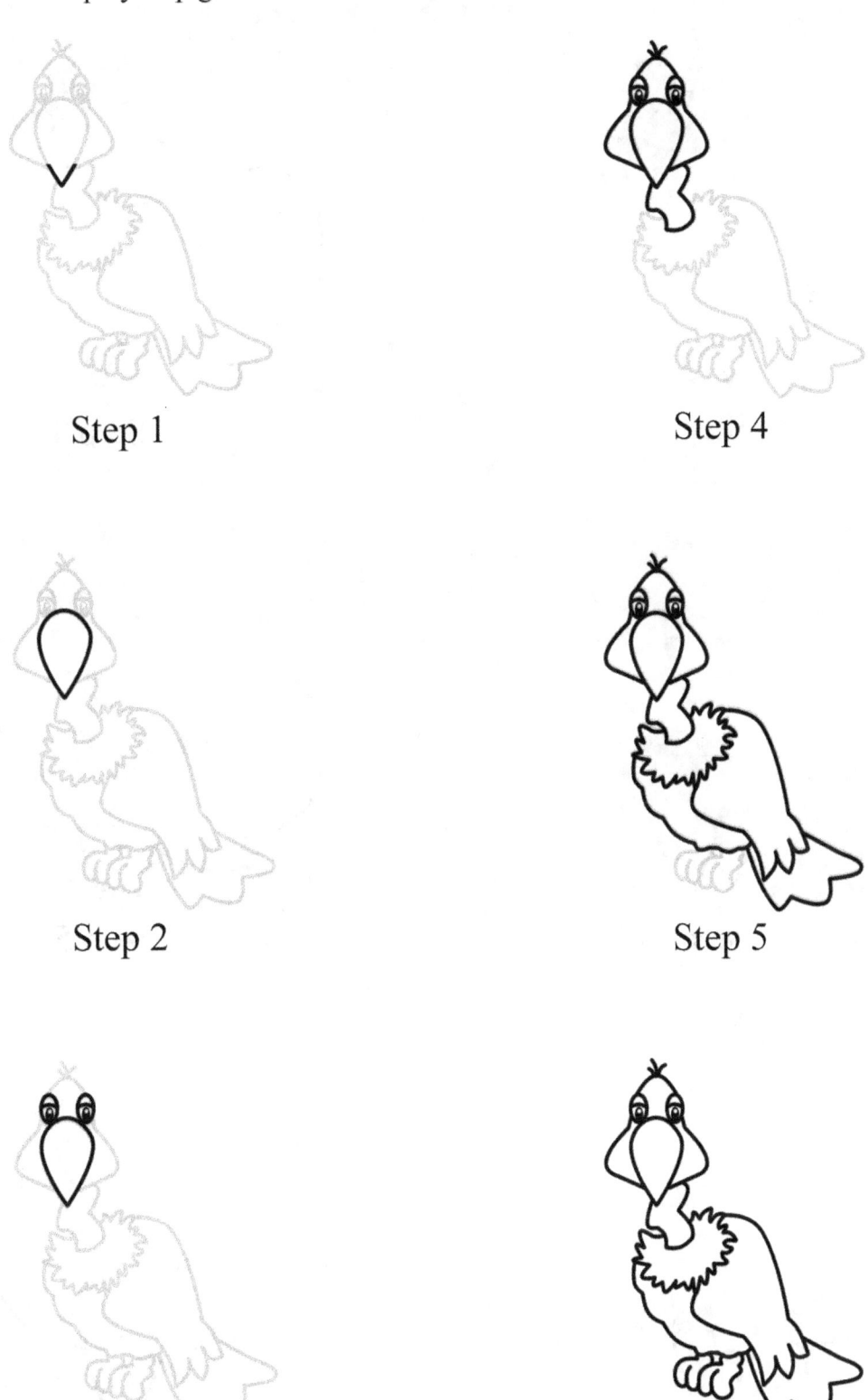

Step 1

Step 2

Step 3

Step 4

Step 5

Step 6

Step by step guide to transform the letter **W** into a **Whale**.

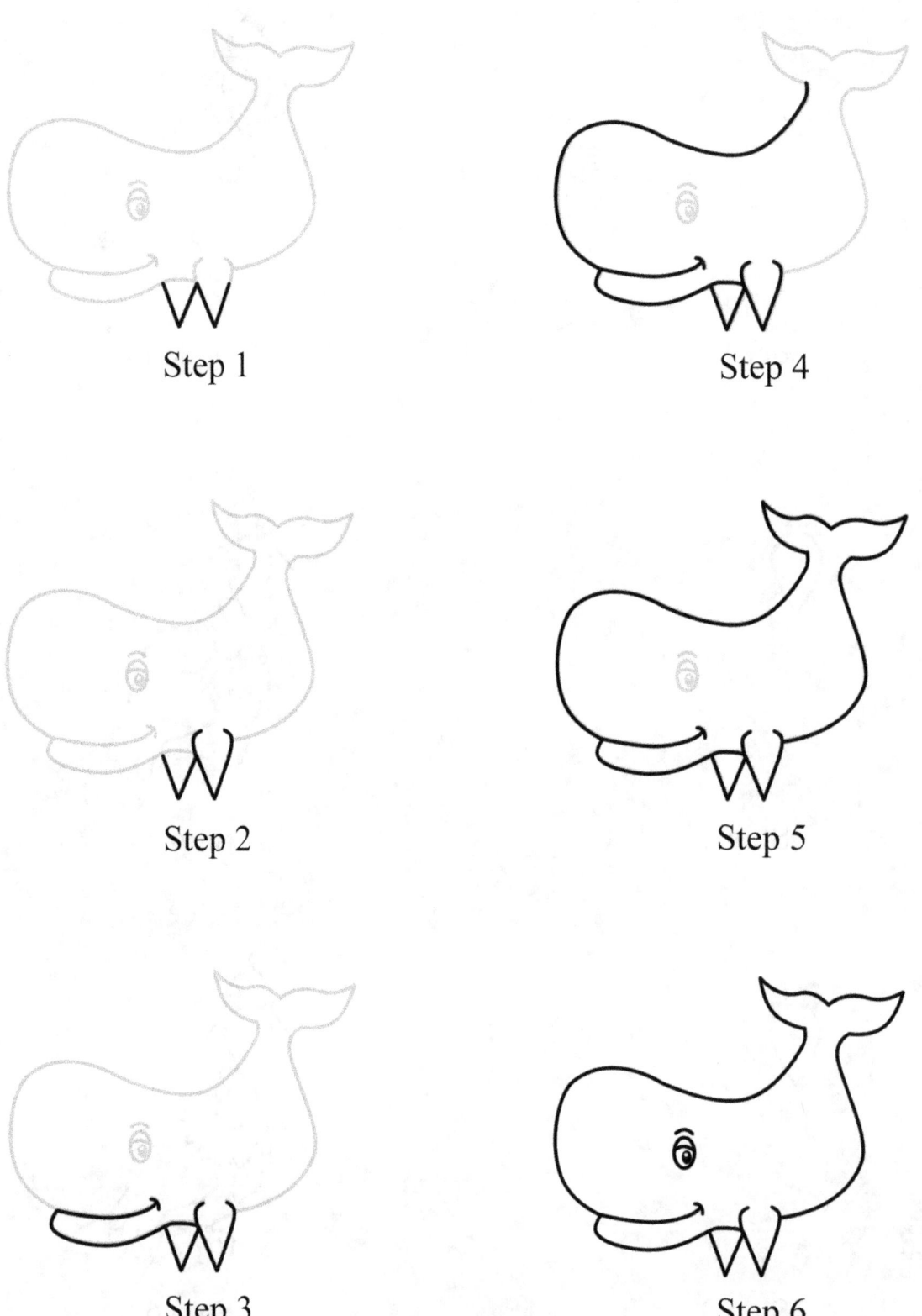

Step 1

Step 2

Step 3

Step 4

Step 5

Step 6

Step by step guide to transform the letter **X** into a **Xylophone**.

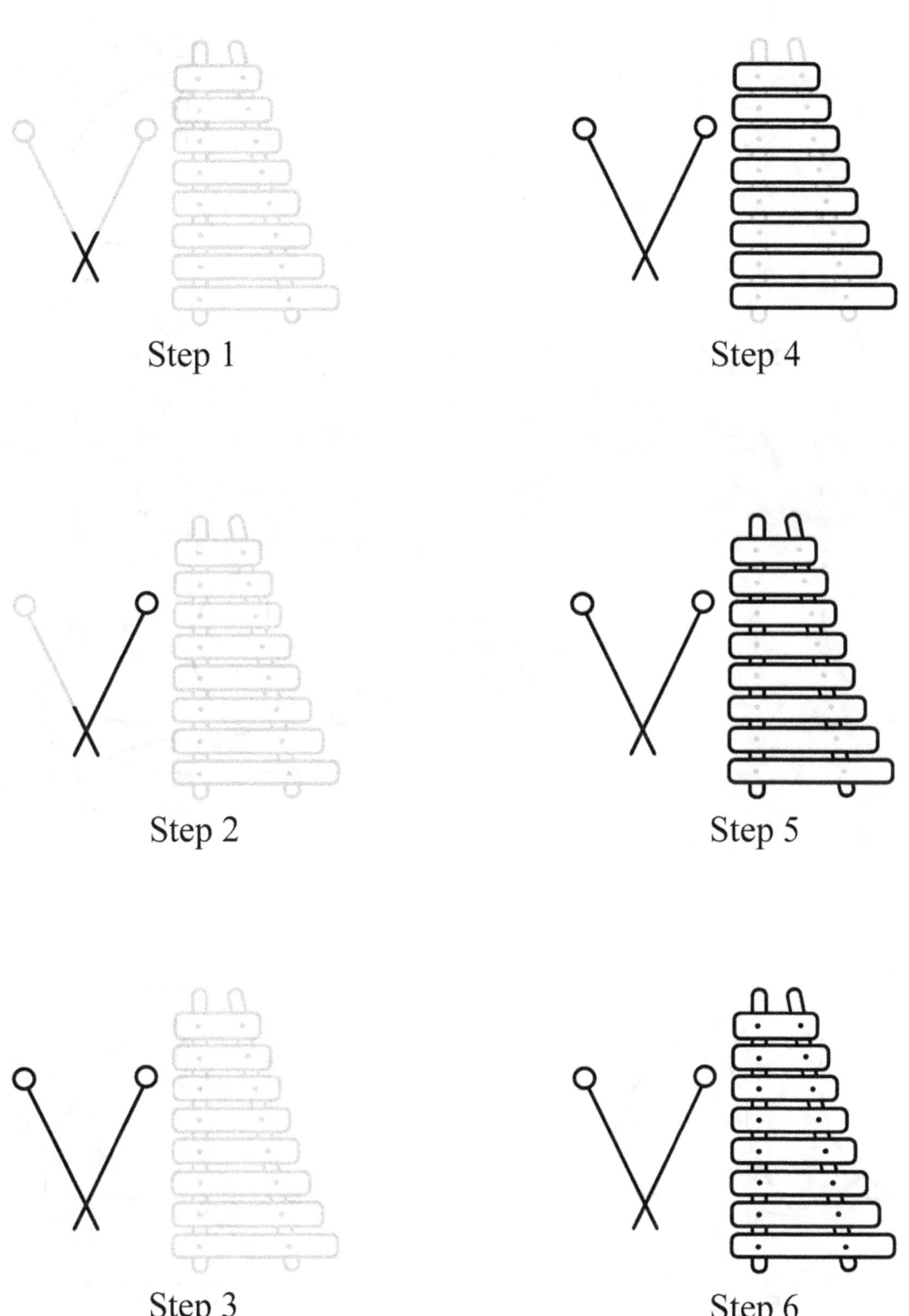

Step 1

Step 2

Step 3

Step 4

Step 5

Step 6

Step by step guide to transform the letter **Y** into a **Yacht**.

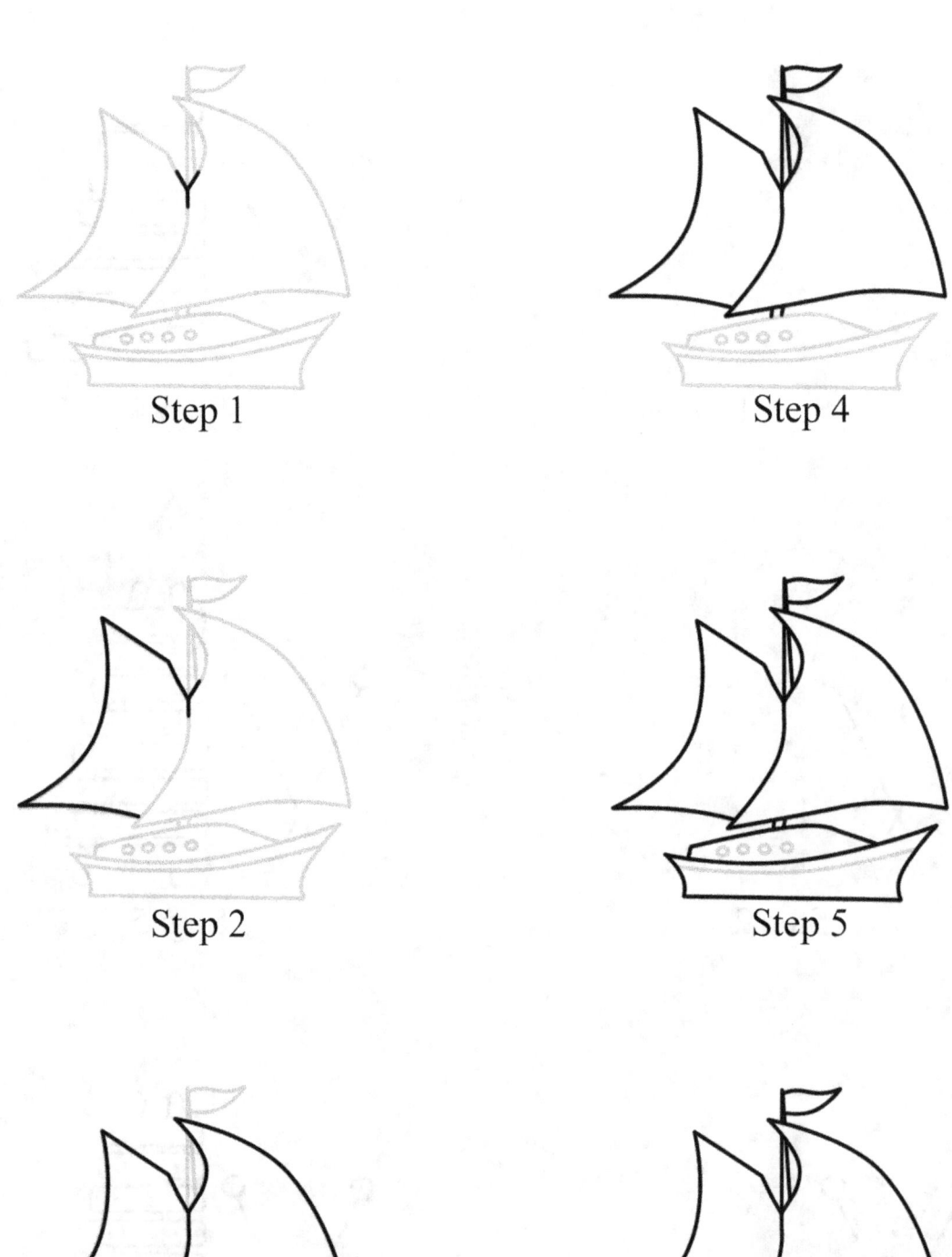

Step 1

Step 2

Step 3

Step 4

Step 5

Step 6

Step by step guide to transform the letter **Z** into a **Zipper**.

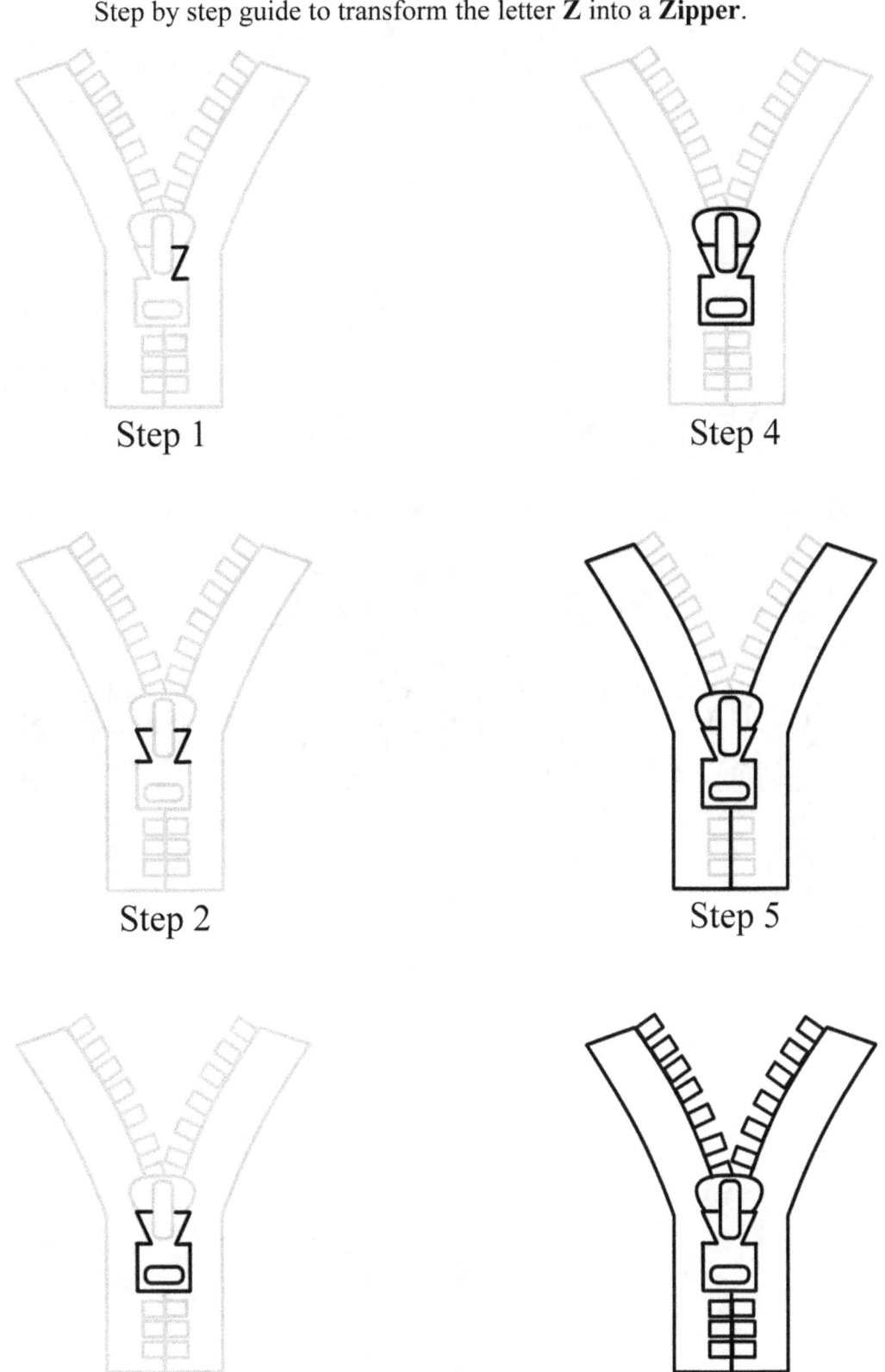

Step 1

Step 2

Step 3

Step 4

Step 5

Step 6

Learn To Transform
Letters Into Drawings

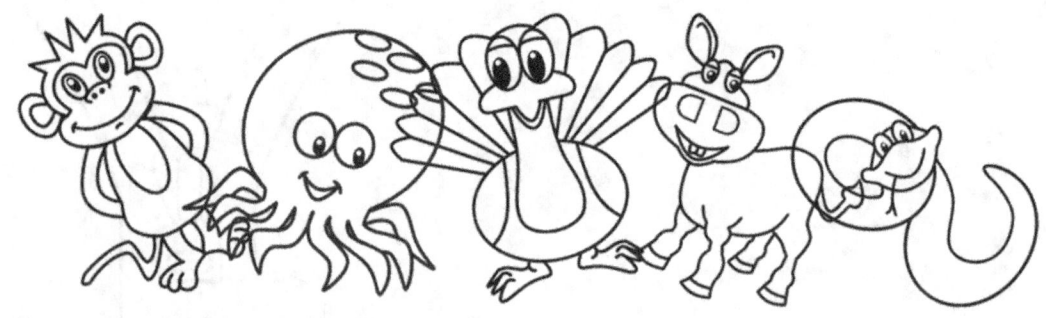

www.ingramcontent.com/pod-product-compliance
Lightning Source LLC
Chambersburg PA
CBHW080859170526
45158CB00009B/2777